6 PM

by

Liz Coronado Castillo

ISBN-978-0-578-68033-0

Library of Congress Control Number: 2020908433
Printed in the United States of America

To my friends and family who have always believed in me

I know you're scared
I'm scared too
Let's love each other anyways

Love often comes at inconvenient times. Don't be so busy you miss it

I want so desperately to believe in love
In soulmates
In timing
In fate
In the power of the universe

I watched as a guy smiled at his phone in the gym today
Such happiness
I texted you right away

Our
First
Kiss

If you could see what I saw, you would be like, "damn"!

Do you think of me
Like I think of you
Do you miss me
Like I miss you
I torture myself like this every day

Will you love me
For all that I am
For all that I am not
Can I tell you my secrets
My fears
My hopes
My dreams
Will you love me
For who I really am

You make me feel so alive
I breathe in your love and exhale hope
You are a Sunday cruise in a lowrider
You are paletas on a hot summer day
You are a cobija San Marcos in the dead of winter
You are love

Anywhere
Any time
Doing anything
As long as it's with you...

Stop
Just stop
Listen for a moment
Your heart is trying to tell you something
Listen to your heart
Fuck everyone else

She said she couldn't love me the way I deserved to be loved
She was right

Don't ever let go, you whispered
I did
It haunts me everyday

I would reach out for you in the middle of the night and hold you

I would be present and, in the moment, when I kissed you, slowly, passionately

I knew one day I would cherish these memories

I knew one day these memories would be all I had left of you

I loved you and you hurt me, so I loved you even more

Your love is simply gone
As fast as a snowflake in West Texas

You left me as the leaves began to fall
Fall turned to winter
I never saw spring that year

The winter seemed longer and colder
She spent it inside
Inside her home
Inside herself

Your memory flows through me like fire
But I don't hate the pain of missing you
It reminds me of the love we once had

Every time I think my heart can't break anymore
It does
And while at this moment I can't conceivably see how
something so shattered can be repaired
I stand here
Defiantly
Not allowing myself to be hardened by it all
Defiantly, I still believe in love

I wonder what your life is like
How do you fill your days
Do you laugh often
I miss it
Your laugh
So carefree
So contagious
So you

I cannot hate you
Once I have let you into my heart you will always have a place
there

I miss our quiet moments together
Being comfortable and happy in complete peace and quiet
with you was a blessing
My soul misses your soul

The first moment we met I felt our souls smile
I never thought you would become just a memory

If I could snap my fingers and forget you, forget all this pain, dry all these tears, I wouldn't
I took a chance on love and I would do it again

I love you so much
But I can't tell you
I miss you so much
But I can't tell you
I will always love you
But I will never be able to tell you

And still I love you
Because you deserve love like I deserve love
You may not be able to love me back and that is ok
Loving someone is an act of strength

Maybe we'll see each other again
Years from now
Healed
Better versions of ourselves

Hearing your voice
After so long
It was what my soul needed

I stand here in front of you with an open heart
I'm terrified
But here I am

Mind: Don't do it!
Heart: DO IT!!! I LOVE BEING IN LOVE! YAY!

I want to love you
I want to give you flowers and bring you coffee
I want to write you silly notes, and romantic notes, and grocery lists
I want to take walks and discover new places
I want you

Your smile is contagious
Your laugh, intoxicating
Your spirit, inspiring
And your touch, invigorating
I may just be addicted

If my life was a romantic comedy you would be my happy ending

Love her with all you got
Let her be the boss
Let her drive your truck
Let her eat your food when she said she wasn't hungry
Open every door for her
Hold her hand
Kiss her forehead
Love her with all you got
Cause you may not always get the chance

I said
I am hard to love
I don't want hard
She replied

You promised to always love me
You promised to love me at the height of my success and in my darkest moments
Then my dark moments came...

I don't love you like you love me, she said
You have a sacrificial love for me, she continued
I thought that's what love was supposed to be
She nodded no and walked away
But I thought you were supposed to love with all your heart...

She handed me back my heart along with my house key

I said I'd call
I knew I wouldn't
She said she'd stay in touch
She knew she wouldn't
It was goodbye forever

My soul let out a silent scream the day you left
I am forced to mourn you while you still walk this earth

She loved me during the Spring but couldn't handle my Winter

I had so many things I wanted to say to you as you walked
away
I love you
Don't do it
Don't leave me
Now they're just empty pleas tattooed all over my heart

I won't beg you to stay
No matter how much my heart hates me for it

I am stronger than you think
So, go on
Leave

I sat in the empty house on the first night in complete silence
The neighborhood was alive with sounds outside
Inside, my heart was crying out your name

The first Saturday morning was hard
The silence scared me

I had no reason to get up but the reason to lay in bed all morning was gone

The owl is back
Right outside my window
He calls out
But you're already gone
He warned me

You rejected me and all of a sudden, I was five again
Feeling unwanted
A disappointment

I don't understand it
So, I create different narratives in my head
One worse than the other

I let all my walls down
I loved you unconditionally
I showed you my truth
You called me weak
Am I though
Are you sure it's me

My chest feels hollow
My heart no longer there
I gave it to you

I don't know what a life without you looks like
I know I gotta do it...but I'm scared

I run my errands
Though I don't want to
I have no choice
Grocery shopping is the loneliest

When I wake up in the morning the first thing I crave is the next night
When I sleep I escape the pain that holds me down every day
That doesn't let me breathe
That makes me question who I am
Then you find me there
In my dreams
You look different each time
I wonder if that's what you look like now

You left me
Why won't you leave my dreams

I wake up...sad, heartbroken
I think about all the things you said to me
All the hurtful words
I fight all day to overcome them
And I do
Then I have to start all over the next day
And the next day
And the next

I gave you all of me
And was willing to accept some of you
I thought some of you was better than none of you

I thought I could shed all my armor in front of you
I could have never imagined you would have used what you
saw against me

The tragedy is that I told you how you could hurt me

I look into the mirror and see all the things you criticized
Your words broke me
I am just a shell of myself
But I am not completely gone...

I want to lay in bed all day
In complete darkness
I hate the light
It reminds me of you

I loved all your faults
Why couldn't you love mine

I knew you didn't love me
I just didn't want to accept that
That's my fault
I did this to myself

I ask the señora to give me a limpia
I ask her to erase your memory from my heart
It hasn't worked yet

I've spent a fortune in candles
Praying for you to leave my dreams

I sit in my driveway each evening
Avoiding the emptiness inside my house
No longer a home

I rearrange things at night
From one place to another
But it will never feel like home
It will never feel like you

I sit in my house in silence for as long as I can
Facing my fears
Afraid to be alone forever
Afraid no one will ever love me
All of me
So I sit
In silence

This must be brujería
You loved me then you didn't

I feel like screaming
I feel like falling to my knees
I feel like giving up
So I stand
I just stand still while the storm rages on
All I can manage right now is to stay standing up

Depression
My head hurts
So much
It feels heavy
Like it's not meant for my body

I'm not present
I hear them talking
But I don't understand
I'm sorry, can you repeat that
Forgive me, say that again
I hold on
But for what

I couldn't get out of bed today
The emptiness was overwhelming
I'll try again tomorrow

I light candles each night
I pray to the angels and saints
Give me peace
I pray to my ancestors
Give me strength
I pray to my abuela
Keep her away from my dreams

I light my candle and say my prayer
Please Virgencita, help me make it one more day

My heart wants to hope
To wait for your return
I tell it no
Stop
It won't

Today was a moment to moment day
That's all I could live

I'm the funniest when it hurts the most
I laugh so that I don't cry

I got into a fight with my heart today
It just doesn't want to accept that you're gone

Your memory caught up to me today

Not understanding why
Not having answers
My heart races
My thoughts rage
I can't breathe
Do I walk it off
Do I stand still
How do I make this go away
How do I make you go away

It's 6:00 PM
I was supposed to be waiting for you to walk down the aisle at
this very moment
I should have kept the cake

This shit cut so deep, I cried in Spanish

How long does it take to get used to not wearing your ring

I knew you would burn me but the fire in your eyes
mesmerized me

Me perdí en tu amor y cuando me lo quitaste me quedé perdida

Lloré ayer
Lloré hoy
Lloraré mañana
Quizás lloraré toda mi vida por tu amor

This heartache is so deep that not even country music will do
Dame una botella y la música de Chente

Como te olvido
Dime mi vida...como lo hiciste tu

Creía que eras mi amor eterno
No se cómo explicarle a mi corazón que no era cierto
Mi pobre corazón simplemente no puede entender

I dreamt that you left
I woke up looking for you
Then I remembered
You left

I wake up every morning
Then I remember
You're gone
I choke back the tears
I want to scream but I swallow it
I get up
Because I have to
I get up

Mis sueños se han convertido a pesadillas

I didn't listen to music for weeks after you left
How could I
Every song reminded me of you

There's a scream trapped deep within my soul

This toxic masculinity that I carry with me is drowning me
But I won't let go of it cause you won't let go of it
I guess I'll drown

I want to be angry I said
Why he said
Because somehow anger makes me feel stronger than sadness

I have moments of resiliency
Moments of clarity
How I wish those moments would last

I see the little green light
There you are
On the other side of the screen
So close, yet so far away

With one press of a button she deleted me from her life
Somehow that hurt more than I could have imagined

You used to share your hopes and dreams with me
Now you don't even share your newsfeed

How much of it was a lie
The first kiss
The 5th
The last...

My dear heart, please stop crying
It will all be over in time

Eventually you have to let go, heart

I was careless with my heart
Dear heart, please forgive me
I am so sorry

I forget everything these days
What I did yesterday
What I had for dinner last night
What I'm supposed to do tomorrow
But somehow, I can't forget you

I never told my friends what I was going through
I never reached out for help
I knew they would hate you
I loved you too much for that

I allowed you to shake my confidence
I questioned my definition of strength
Now, I need to repair myself
I need to redefine myself
No one can give me back what I let you take

Time will heal you, they say
It's just going to take time, they say
I'm drowning in time, I reply

My mom says God doesn't give you more than you can handle
Por favor Diosito, ya no puedo

How can I forget you when my steps in this empty house echo your name

Prendo mis velas cada noche y rezo
Siempre en español
Para que mi abuela que está en el cielo me pueda escuchar
Le pido al Santo Niño de Atocha que me ayude
No para que regreses
Pero que dejes de visitar me en mis sueños
Ya, déjame

My dog walks around this empty house looking for you
Looking for the kids
Looking for his brother
You broke my damn dog's heart

They say you can't die from a broken heart, but my chest burns
with sorrow
I find it hard to breathe
I pray to all the angels and saints to get me through the pain
I light candles for the love that was lost
The light glowing in the dark helps me sleep

I lost myself in loving you
I don't know where to start looking
How did I become this woman

I looked for love in your eyes
I found pain
And a fire burning so hot I knew it would burn me some day

The scar you left on my heart may never heal
A constant reminder of what was

I live for moments
Moments when I'm actually there
Present
In it
Most of the time my body is there
But my spirit
My heart
My mind
Are not
I'm thinking why aren't I happy
I have everything I need
I'm good
But the truth is
I'm not
I'm only good for a moment

The memories come in waves
At times so real and so hard they take my breath away
So, I close my eyes to remember
And I send you love

Survive
Some days I have to whisper that to myself
Some days survive is all I got
Survive, I say to myself
Survive 'til you can stand up and thrive
Just survive

Sometimes I have dark moments
Moments so dark I can't even see tomorrow
I hold onto my abuela's prayers for me
I hold onto any piece of hope I can find in the darkness
Any of the tiniest of light
I hold on
And that's what matters
I hold on...

I thought I could write you out of my heart
I thought I could write you out of my heart
I thought I could write you out of my heart
I thought I could write you out of my heart
I thought I could write you out of my heart
I thought I could write you out of my heart
I thought I could write you out of my heart
I thought I could write you out of my heart

A day living in the present
Just one day
No memories, no fears, no anxiety
I just want one day

You don't deserve my kindness
You don't deserve my kindness
But my heart doesn't know that
I extend to you all the love and compassion that you withheld
from me
Don't mistake my kindness for weakness

My soul was shattered into so many pieces
I didn't even know how to begin to rebuild it
I would look in the mirror hoping to find a piece of me
Any little piece of me that was recognizable

I don't even recognize your face anymore
How could I have loved you so much
Where did that person go
Where did I go

I loved you so much that I stopped loving myself
I don't know what hurts more
You breaking my heart or me breaking my heart

I wear a smile cause frowning will only age me
No matter how heartbroken I am
I still gotta look good

I love you
That's all
I love you

I look around this gym and all I see are broken hearts
We trade one pain for another

I don't know when I'll ever laugh again
That silent, tears, can't catch my breath laugh
I just don't know

My blessing is my curse
I see so much beauty in this world I want to burst
I feel so much pain in this world I want to burst
My blessing is my curse

I woke up today and thought of you
Maybe tomorrow
Maybe tomorrow will be the day that I forget you

Hope is such a complicated thing
At times lifesaving
And at times, it's a foolish, foolish thing

If I could only keep one memory it would be our first kiss

You are paradoxically the water that quenches my thirst
And the fire that causes the drought

My soul whispers "It will be ok"
While my heart cries itself to sleep

I wanted to grow old with you
Since you left, I've aged a lifetime

I've tried to erase you so many times
But there you are
In my thoughts
In my dreams

Anoche te soñé
Anoche te amé
Anoche...

I miss the beat of your heart next to mine
The way you rested your head on my chest
Your warm skin next to mine
My soul misses your soul

Sometimes I get tripped up by a sudden memory of you
A smell takes me back to the first day
I see your smile, clearly, like you never left
I cherish the moment
Then set it free...

Your memory knocked the air out of me today
I took a moment
Sat with the pain
Then I smiled defiantly and went on about my day

I love being in love
It's the pinche broken heart I could do without

In that moment I forgot everything
All the pain
All the sorrow
In that moment
Singing at the top of my lungs to Whitney Houston with the windows open
I needed that moment

Some days I am so consumed by so much sadness
Simply getting out of bed is a victory
Somedays I feel so amazing I don't want to go to bed

Our love was built out of sand
The same sand I knew the tides would come and wash away

That feeling I got when my phone beeped and I knew it was
you
I miss that shit
Your fucked-up hair in the morning
I miss that shit
Your smile
I miss that shit
The heartache you caused me
I could've done without that shit

Your love was fleeting and now I am learning to find peace with the impermanence of it all

I don't know why I'm crying anymore
Because you left me
Or because you treated me so bad

I still miss the you I thought you were
It's my own fantasies that are breaking my heart

Wednesday
You told me you didn't love me on a Wednesday
You moved out on a Wednesday
Wednesday
I will forever be getting over Wednesday

I surrender to the pain
They say fighting it makes it worse
I'm too tired to fight
I let the pain rush my soul
I cry, quietly
Not fighting it

Tonight, I called the suicide hotline
Then went to the gym

I deleted your last voicemail today
Love of my life, where are you, you said

I read your last letter
For the last time

I did not give up today
I can't promise tomorrow
But not today

I
Did
Not
Cry
Today

It was an ordinary day
Nothing special
The past came up from behind and knocked me to my knees
I said to my past, "I see you"
I got up, made sure nobody saw and kept on walking

We found our way back to each other
And it wasn't meant to be...again
And that's the end of it
There's no more romanticizing your love

I love myself
Now I just have to look in the mirror and believe it

I fell in love with you
I fell
I let go
I didn't hold back
I'm not ashamed of that

I am enough
I look into the mirror
Tears still in my eyes
I do my best not to let them fall out
I whisper "I am enough"

Believe in yourself
Believe your intuition
You're not crazy
Don't let them make you think that

A fool is not one who loves but one who cannot

She was broken
She didn't mean to pass on her trauma
But she did
And I was on the receiving end

You don't deserve to be hated
You deserve to be loved
I hope you let someone someday

Pues...ni modo

The kindest thing you ever did for me was to leave

I have survived all that this life has thrown at me
I will survive you

You may not love me, but I am loved
Maybe you had to break my heart for me to open my eyes
To the love that surrounds me

I knew I would be okay when the silence of an empty house no longer scared me

By the time you decide to look back at what you left
You'll find I'm way ahead of you

I spent all this time wishing you would change instead of changing myself

I do not expect anything in return
I will just love you
I got this one

Letting go of you...
How can I
How can I not...
Who am I to stop you
Go be free and wild
Like your heart

Then there comes a day when you just move on
No more memories first thing in the morning
No breakdowns when you walk into your empty house at night
No Adele on repeat
Like a Spring day you are reborn

I've known darkness and for that I am grateful
How else would I know my own strength

If you're this amazing in pieces,
I can't imagine how phenomenal you will be
Once you feel whole

She's the kinda girl who won't write in her book with pen because she's afraid of the permanence but is covered in tattoos

May your day be bright
May you feel energized in all you do
May no fucks be given

You are a garden
Plant your seeds of positivity
Work hard every day
Love yourself
You will be happy you did

Tatted and educated
Chola and scholar
Mexican and American
I am an act of resistance

I have dreams bigger than you, bigger than me, bigger than anything I've known
I dream so hard I scare myself
I may not know when I'll achieve my dreams but I will
I wake up every day because I have dreams

I choose love
Every time

Que paso guerita
I thought you were down with my raza
You can make love to my brown body
But not live in my brown hood
You can't find gluten free tortillas at la tiendita
How sad
Go colonize another body

You're drowning, you said
I can't go down with you, you said
And I was
But I didn't
And here I am

Quiero morir soñando

THE END
(YA ESTUVO)

Made in the USA
Columbia, SC
21 May 2020